Authentic
GUITAR-TAB
Edition ™
Includes Complete Solos

sublime

CONTENTS

D1399275

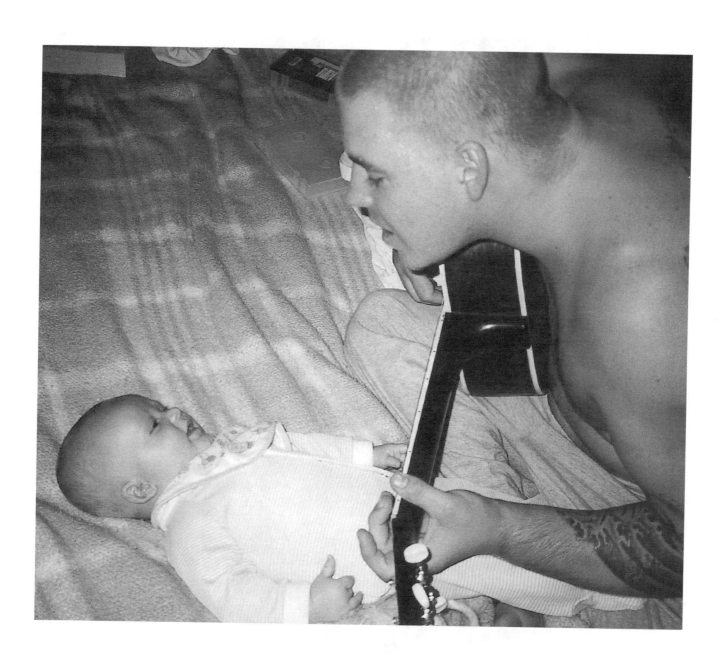

Garden Grove

Words and Music by Brad Nowell, Eric Wilson, Floyd Gaugh and Linton Johnson

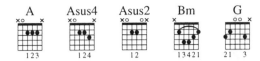

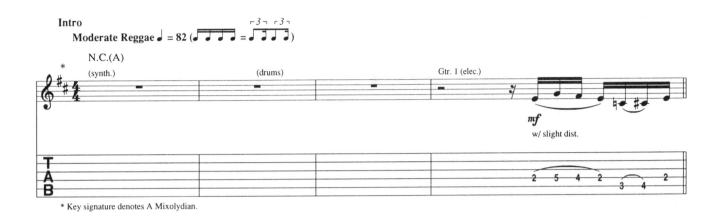

MCA music publishing

dog.   All that I can see, I   steal. _   I   fill up   my   ga-rage, _   'cause in my   mind, _

Bridge
Gtr. 1 tacet
N.C.(A)

mu - sic   from   Ja - mai - ca,   all   the   love   that   I   found. ___   Pull

o - ver,   there's   a   rea - son   why   my   soul's ___   un - sound. _   4. It's

Verse

you.   It's that   shit   stuck un-der my   shoe,   it's that   smell in-side the   van. _   It's my   bed sheet cov-ered with

* Sung behind the beat.

sand,   sit-ting through a   shit-ty   band.   Get-tin'   dog   shit   on   my   hands,   get-tin'   has-sled   by   the

sim.

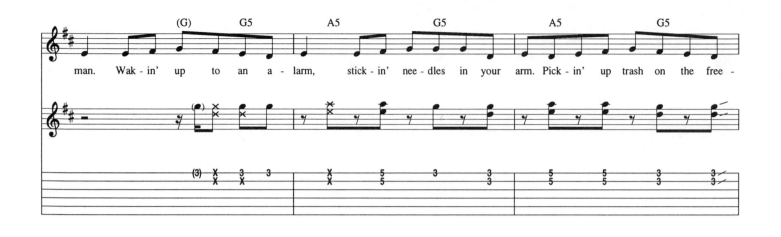

man. Wak - in' up to an a - larm, stick - in' nee - dles in your arm. Pick - in' up trash on the free -

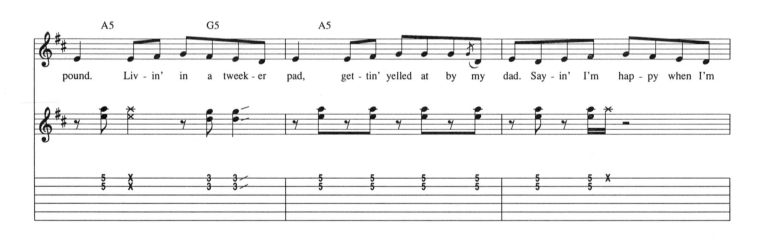

way, feel - in' de - pressed ev - er - y day. Leav - in' with - out mak - in' a sound, pick - in' my dog up at the

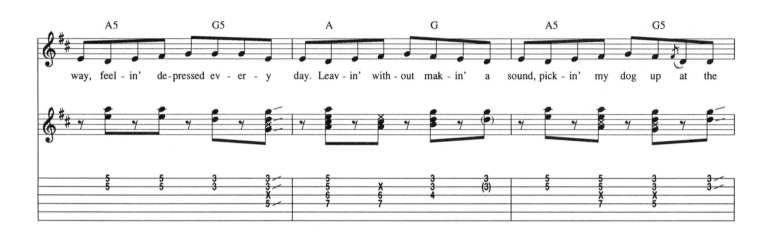

pound. Liv - in' in a tweek - er pad, get - tin' yelled at by my dad. Say - in' I'm hap - py when I'm

Chorus

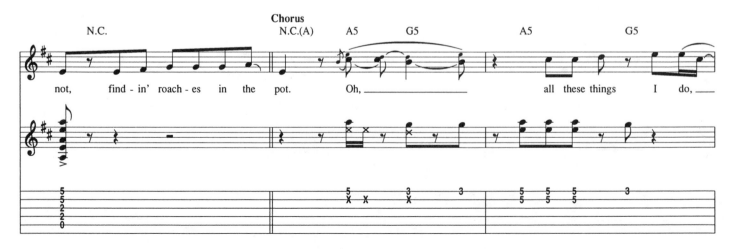

not, find - in' roach - es in the pot. Oh, _____ all these things I do, _____

10

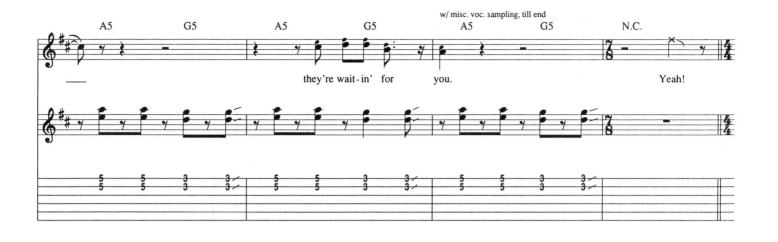

they're wait-in' for you. Yeah!

Interlude

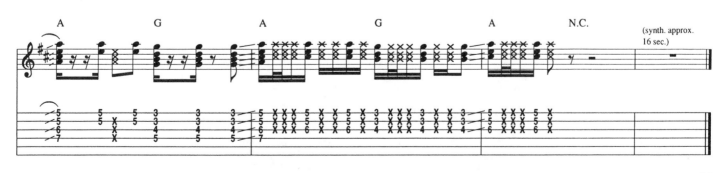

What I Got

Words and Music by Brad Nowell, Eric Wilson and Floyd Gaugh

MCA music publishing

Got to find a rea-son why my mon-ey's all gone. ___ I ___ got a Dal-ma-tion, and

I can still __ get high. __ I ___ can play the gui-tar like a moth-er-fuck-in' ri-ot.

Gtr. 2 (acous.)

Fill 1

End Fill 1

f

End Riff A

Gtr. 1

P.S. _ _ _ _ *

* Pick slide unintentionally sounds open strings.

Interlude

w/ Voc. ad lib.
Gtr. 1: w/ Riff A, 1st 4 meas. only, simile

2. Well, life

Gtr. 2

grad. bend
1/4

let ring

3/4

** Tap gtr. body

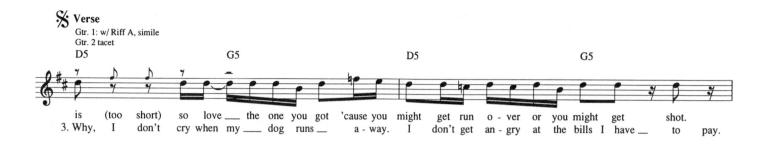

Verse

Gtr. 1: w/ Riff A, simile
Gtr. 2 tacet

is (too short) so love ___ the one you got 'cause you might get run o - ver or you might get shot.
3. Why, I don't cry when my ___ dog runs ___ a - way. I don't get an - gry at the bills I have ___ to pay.

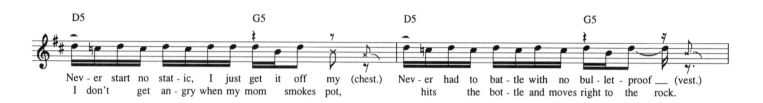

Nev - er start no stat - ic, I just get it off my (chest.) Nev - er had to bat - tle with no bul - let - proof ___ (vest.)
I don't get an - gry when my mom smokes pot, hits the bot - tle and moves right to the rock.

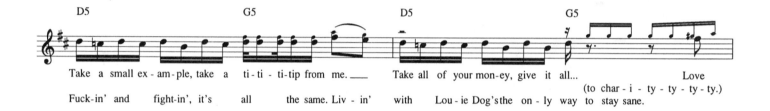

Take a small ex - am - ple, take a ti - ti - ti-tip from me. ___ Take all of your mon-ey, give it all... Love
Fuck-in' and fight-in', it's all the same. Liv - in' with Lou - ie Dog's the on - ly way to stay sane. (to char - i - ty - ty - ty - ty.)

To Coda

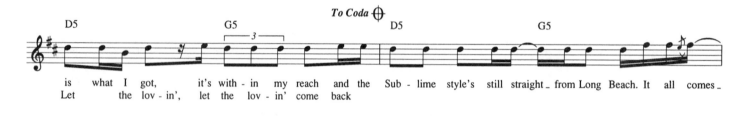

is what I got, it's with - in my reach and the Sub - lime style's still straight ___ from Long Beach. It all comes ___
Let the lov - in', let the lov - in' come back

___ back to you, you fin - 'ly get what you de - serve. Try and test that, you're bound to get served.

Gtr. 2: w/ Fill 1

Love's what I got, don't start a ri - ot. You feel it when the dance gets hot.

Chorus

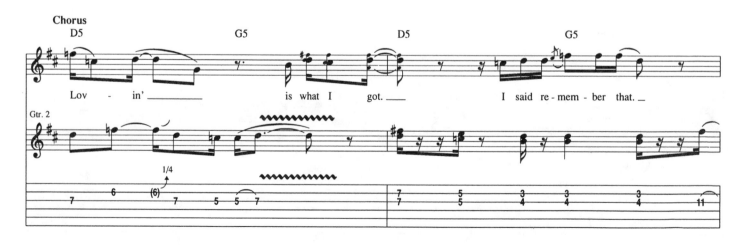

Lov - in' ___ is what I got. ___ I said re - mem - ber that. ___

Gtr. 2

1/4

Wrong Way

Words and Music by Brad Nowell, Eric Wilson and Floyd Gaugh

Verse
Moderately ♩ = 116

1. An-nie's twelve years old; in two more she'll be a whore. No-bod-y ev-er told her it's the

Gtr. 1 (slight dist.)

let ring

* Key signature denotes E Mixolydian.   ** Chord symbols reflect implied tonality.

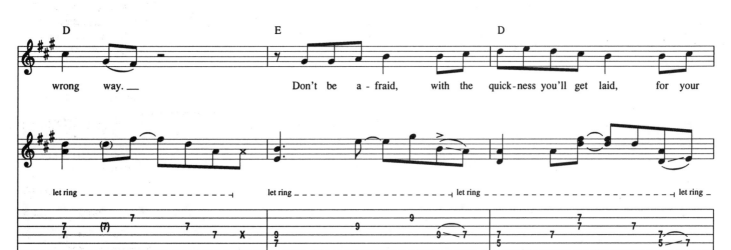

wrong way. — Don't be a-fraid, with the quick-ness you'll get laid, for your

let ring

fam-i-ly get paid. It's the wrong way. —   2. I gave her all that I had to give. —

Verse
Faster ♩ = 148

Rhy. Fig. 1

let ring

* Key signature denotes A Mixolydian.

MCA music publishing

* Key signature denotes F♯ Mixolydian.

* Key signature denotes B Mixolydian.

Same in the End

Words and Music by Brad Nowell, Eric Wilson, Floyd Gaugh

MCA music publishing

Get down on your knees and ___ start to pray, ___ oh. ____
___ can see for miles and ___ miles and miles, _ oh. ____

Gtr. 2: w/ Fill 1

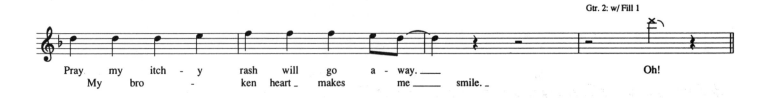

Pray my itch - y rash will go a - way. ___ Oh!
My bro - ken heart _ makes me ___ smile. _

Pre-Chorus
Gtr. 1 tacet
Gtr. 2: w/ Rhy. Fig. 2, simile

F5	C5/G	A5	D5/A	C5	B♭5

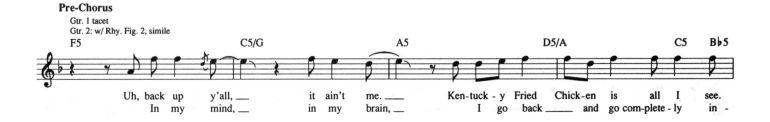

Uh, back up y'all, ___ it ain't me. ___ Ken-tuck-y Fried Chick-en is all I see.
In my mind, ___ in my brain, ___ I go back ____ and go com-plete-ly in -

Gtr. 2: w/ Rhy. Fill 1, simile, 1st time
Gtr. 2: w/ Rhy. Fill 2, 2nd time

F5	A5

sane. It's a hell - i - fied way to start ___ your day. ____
It ain't per - s'nal, it ain't me.

Gtr. 2: w/ Rhy. Fig. 2, simile

F5	C5/G	A5	D5/A	C5	B♭5

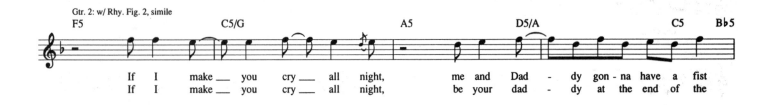

If I make ___ you cry ___ all night, me and Dad - dy gon - na have a fist
If I make ___ you cry ___ all night, be your dad - dy at the end of the

Gtr. 2: w/ Rhy. Fig. 3

F	A5	A

fight. It ain't per - s'nal, it ain't me. ____
night. Take a load ____ from my big gun. ____

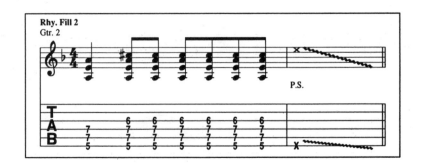

Rhy. Fill 2
Gtr. 2

P.S.

Chorus
Gtr. 2 tacet
Gtr. 1: w/ Rhy. Fig. 4, simile

D/F#   C/E   F/C   D/F#

I on - ly hear what you told _____ me to be. _____ I'm a back -
You on - ly see what you want _____ to be - lieve. _____ When you creep

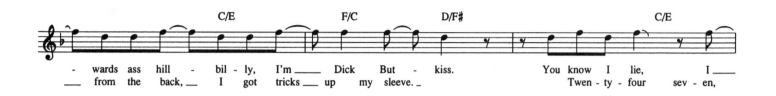

           C/E   F/C   D/F#   C/E

- wards ass hill - bil - ly, I'm _____ Dick But - kiss. You know I lie, I _____
_____ from the back, _____ I got tricks _____ up my sleeve. _____ Twen - ty - four sev - en,

F/C   D/F#   C/E   F/C

_____ get mean. _____ I'm a thief _____ in the dark, _____ I'm a rag - in' ma - chine. _____
dev - il's best friend. Makes no dif - 'rence, it's all _____ same in _____

Guitar Solo

Gtr. 1

Dm   Bb/D   F/C

_____ the end.

Gtr. 3 (dist.)

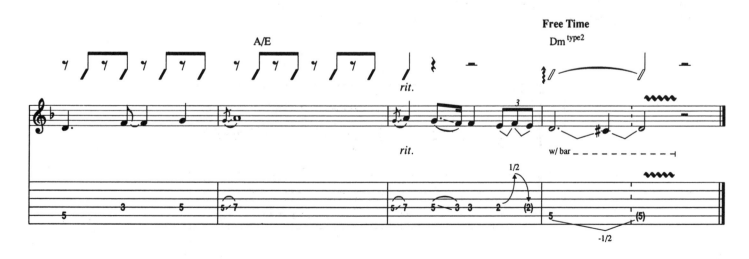

A/E

Free Time

Dm type2

rit.

rit.

w/ bar

1/2

-1/2

25

April 29, 1992 (Miami)

Words and Music by Brad Nowell, Marshall Goodman and Mike Happoldt

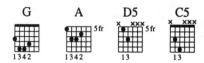

** Sung ahead of the beat.

MCA music publishing

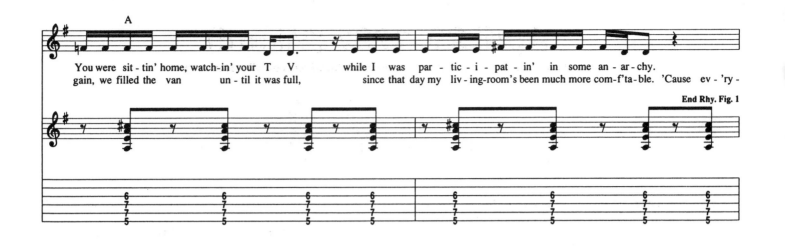

You were sit-tin' home, watch-in' your T V while I was par-tic-i-pat-in' in some an-ar-chy.
gain, we filled the van un-til it was full, since that day my liv-ing-room's been much more com-f'ta-ble. 'Cause ev-'ry-

End Rhy. Fig. 1

Gtr. 2: w/ Rhy. Fig. 1, 2 times

First spot we hit, it was my li-quor store. I fi-nal-ly got all that al-co-hol I can't af-ford. With
bod-y in the hood has had it up to here. It's get-ting hard-er and hard-er and hard-er each and ev-'ry year. Some

red lights flash-in', time __ to re-tire, __ and then we turned that li-quor store in-to a struc-ture fire.
kids went in a store with their moth-er. I saw her when she came out; she was get-tin' some Pamp-ers.

Next stop we hit, it was the mu-sic shop. It on-ly took one brick to make that win-dow drop.
They said it was for the black man, they said it was for the Mex-i-can, and not for the white man. But if you

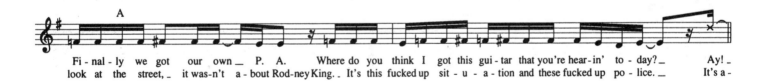

Fi-nal-ly we got our own __ P. A. Where do you think I got this gui-tar that you're hear-in' to-day? __ Ay! __
look at the street, __ it was-n't a-bout Rod-ney King. It's this fucked up sit-u-a-tion and these fucked up po-lice. __ It's a-

1. Interlude

Gtr. 2 tacet
w/ misc. scanner calls

N.C.(D5)

Gtr. 1

P.M. _ _ _ _ | P.M. _ _ _ _ | P.M. _ _ _ _ |

* Piano arr. for gtr.

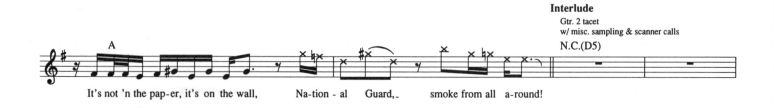

Santeria

Words and Music by Brad Nowell, Eric Wilson and Floyd Gaugh

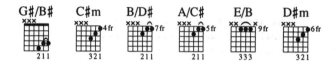

MCA music publishing

San-cho that__ she's found,__ well I'd pop a cap in San-cho and I'd slap her down.____

Chorus

__ But I real-ly wan-na know, ____ ah, ba-by, mm. ____ All I real-ly wan-na say__

let ring throughout

I can't de-fine. Well, it's love__ that I need. ____ 2. Oh, ____ my soul__ will have__ to

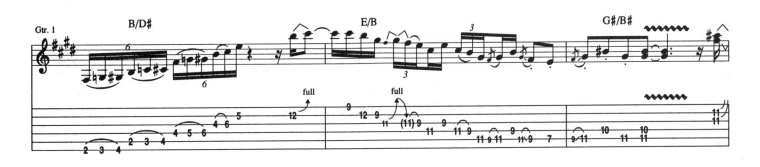

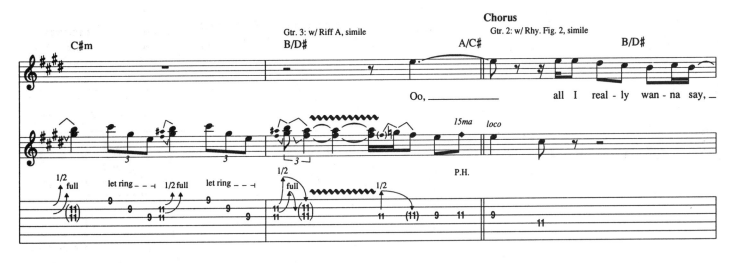

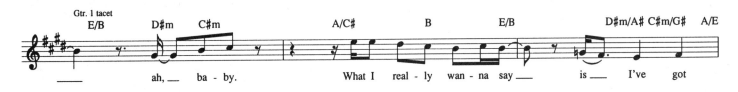

Oo, ___ all I real - ly wan - na say, ___

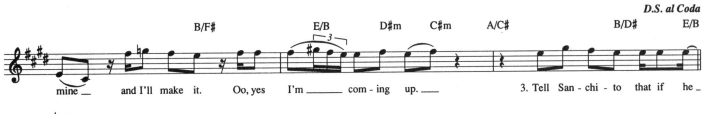

ah, ___ ba - by. What I real - ly wan - na say ___ is ___ I've got

D.S. al Coda

mine ___ and I'll make it. Oo, yes I'm ___ com - ing up. ___ 3. Tell San - chi - to that if he ___

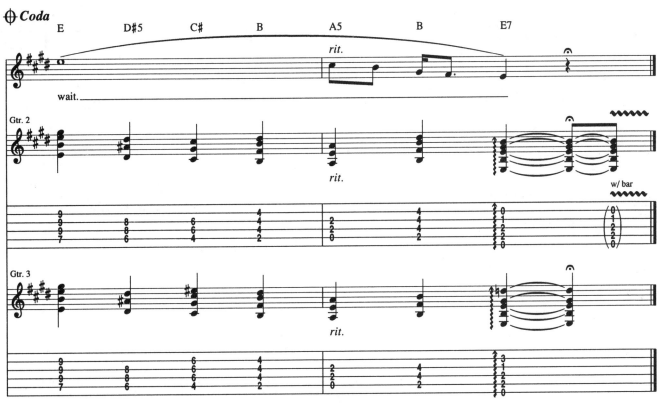

Seed

Words and Music by Brad Nowell, Eric Wilson and Floyd Gaugh

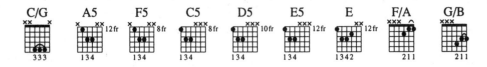

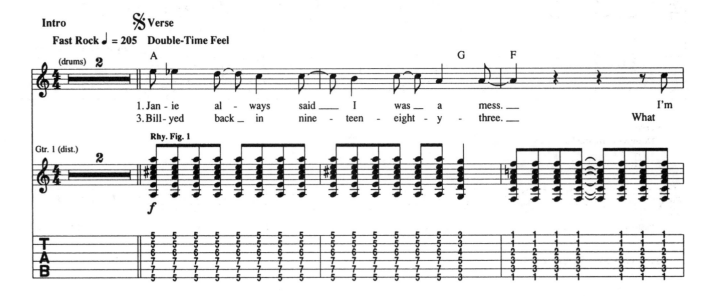

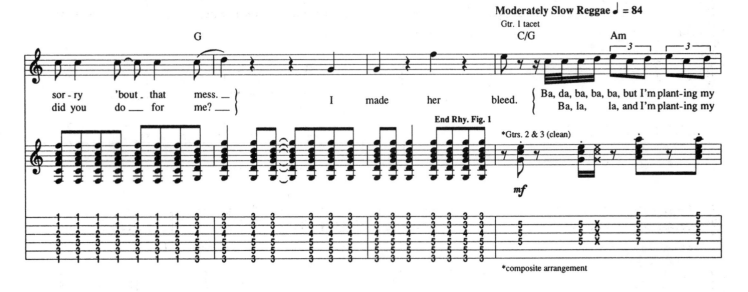

MCA music publishing

Jailhouse

(Anonymous)

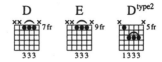

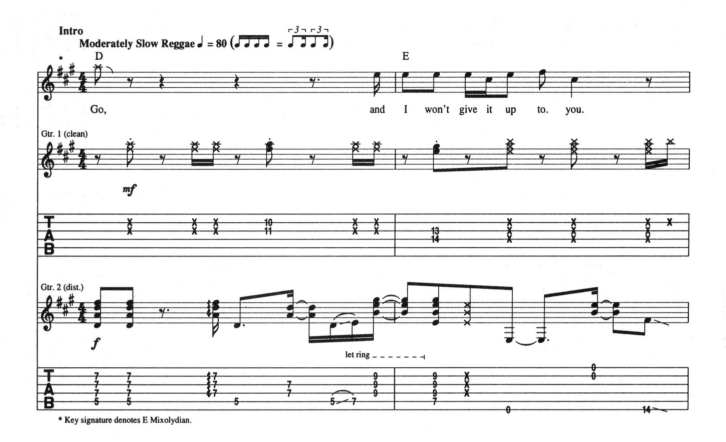

* Key signature denotes E Mixolydian.

E D E
emp - ty, Ru - dy gets plen - ty.
End Rhy. Fig. 1
mf
End Rhy. Fig. 1A
Gtrs. 1 & 2: w/ Rhy. Figs. 1 & 1A, 3 times, simile
D E D E D
The ba-ton stick gets short-er, Ru - dy gets tal - ler. Can't fight a-gainst the youth
E D E
'cause we're strong. Them are rude, rude peo - ple.
D E D
Can't fight a - gainst the youth, 'cause we're strong and we're rude, rude
Verse
Gtr. 2 tacet 1st time; w/ Rhy. Fig. 3, 3 times, 2nd time, simile
Gtr. 1: w/ Rhy. Fig. 1, 6 times, simile
E D
peo - ple. Long, play it a - gain. 2. Now when I was a youth in nine - teen-eight - y - three, was the
when I was a youth it was the best day, it was the
E D
best day of my life. Had the eight - y - nine vi - sion, we did - n't fuss and no fight when
E D
all the lit - tle dar-lin's wan - na be my wife. A vi - sion, it was play - in' on my gui - tar,
When that rhy-thm,

* Played behind the beat.

Verse

3. What I's been _ told _ to the wise   and up-root - ed.   Yeah,   it's gon-na be re-vealed   un - to

babes   and _ Sub - lime. ____   Oo.

pitch: F#

Root - sy, loot - sy, loot - sy. __   Can't fight a - gainst _ the youth _   right now. _

* ① is bumped, then fade out w/ volume knob.

Pawn Shop

Words and Music by Brad Nowell, Eric Wilson and Floyd Gaugh

* Chord symbols reflect overall tonality.

MCA music publishing

Paddle Out

Words and Music by Brad Nowell, Eric Wilson and Floyd Gaugh

(cont. in notation)

steady gliss.

* Trem. pick while sliding down ⑥.

Verse
Slightly Faster ♩ = 208

2. Na - tur - al brid - ges on a clean west swell breaks o - ver the reef __ like a bat out - ta hell. __

Stock - ton Av - e - nue gets hol - low and mean, __ and on a big day it works

like a ma - chine. __ Out - side Stock - ton gets hot like a glove.

Swift Street, John Street, in - to Mit - chell's Cove. Big Steam - er Lane makes you

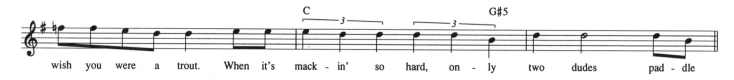

wish you were a trout. When it's mack - in' so hard, on - ly two dudes pad - dle

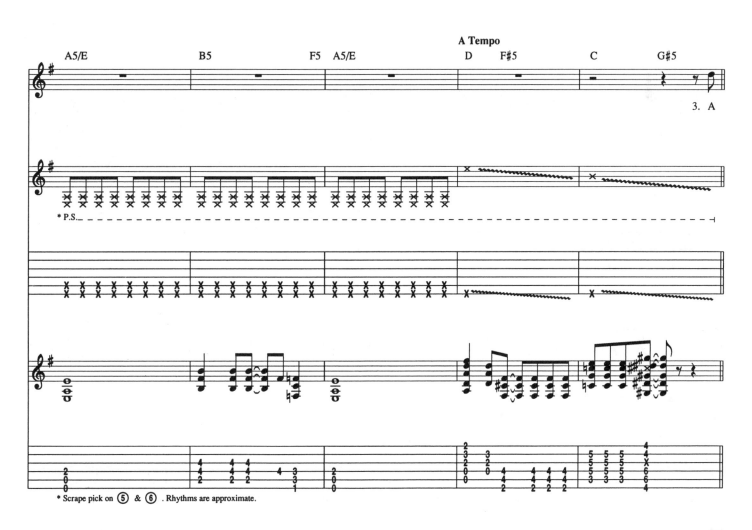

* Scrape pick on ⑤ & ⑥. Rhythms are approximate.

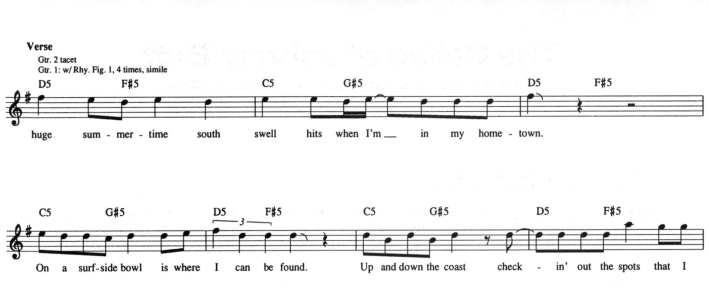

Verse

Gtr. 2 tacet
Gtr. 1: w/ Rhy. Fig. 1, 4 times, simile

huge sum - mer - time south swell hits when I'm __ in my home - town.

On a surf-side bowl is where I can be found. Up and down the coast check - in' out the spots that I

Outro-Guitar Solo

love the most. __

The Ballad of Johnny Butt

Words and Music by Richard Seiga, Kevin Roach and Mike Davis

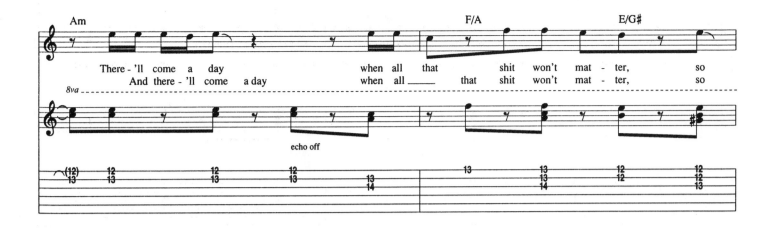

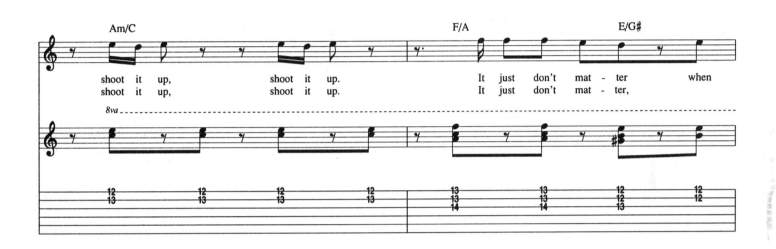

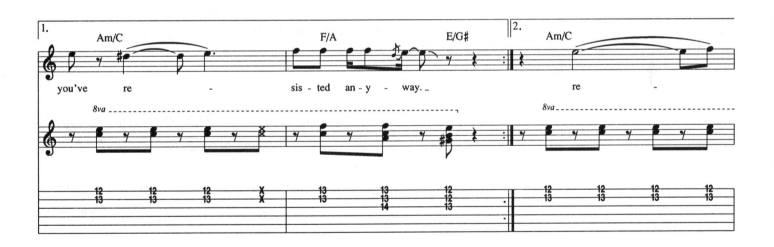

Burritos

Words and Music by Brad Nowell, Eric Wilson and Floyd Gaugh

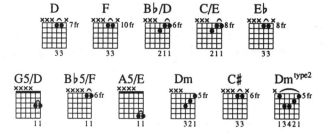

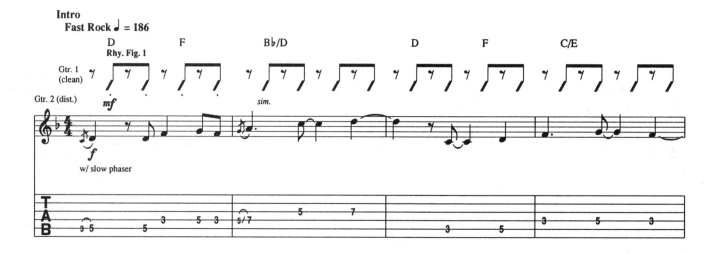

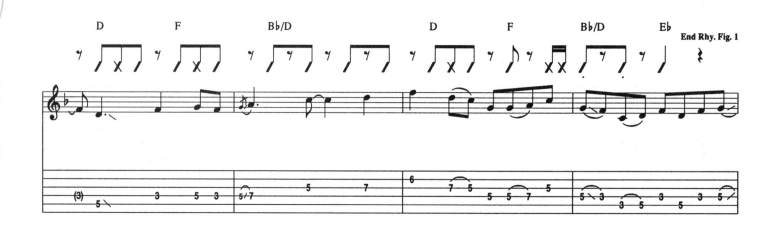

MCA music publishing

* Played behind the beat.

Chorus

Keep on ___ skank - in' Ron - nie, ___ skank the night a - way. ___

But the time is com - ing for us all to pay. Hey!

Coda
Guitar Solo

Chorus

Keep on ___ skank - in' Ron - nie, ___ skank the night a - way. ___

Chorus

Gtr. 1: w/ Rhy. Fig. 3, 1st 7 meas.

Keep on ___ skank-in' Ron-nie, skank the night a-way. ___

But the time is com-ing for us all to pay. Hey!

Outro-Guitar Solo

Slowly ♩ = 76

Hey!

Gtr. 2

let ring _ _ _ _ _ _ _

Gtr. 1

Under My Voodoo

Words and Music by Brad Nowell, Eric Wilson amd Floyd Gaugh

MCA music publishing

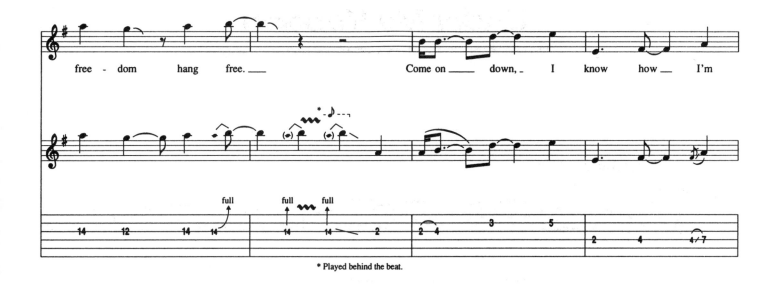

free - dom hang free. __ Come on ___ down, _ I know how _ I'm

* Played behind the beat.

go - ing to make you come here. Don't you know it ain't no thing you de - plore, _ so don't

take more _ than you need. It's some - thing that I do la - ter, now it's o - ver now.

Gtr. 1

let ring ⌐

Gtr. 2 (dist.)

* vol. swell

truth.   It ain't no deal if you wan-na give in _____ like I wan-na

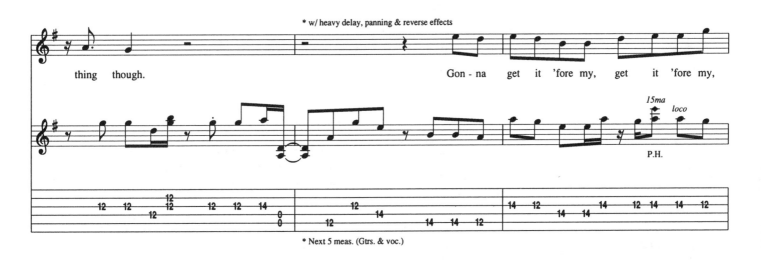

* w/ heavy delay, panning & reverse effects

thing though.   Gon - na get it 'fore my, get it 'fore my,

* Next 5 meas. (Gtrs. & voc.)

get my 'fore it's gone. And I'm gone, it's gone. Got - ta get ya, got, got, got un-der my _ voo -

Chorus

Gtrs. 1 & 2: w/ Rhy. Fig. 1, simile

G5   F#5   F5   E5

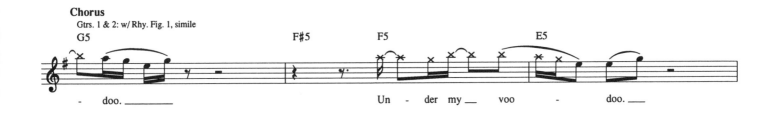

- doo. _____   Un - der my _ voo - doo. _____

It's un - der my _ voo - doo.

Get Ready

Words and Music by Brad Nowell, Eric Wilson and Floyd Gaugh

MCA music publishing

zy fools   wait with their fin - gers crossed for you to break __ the rules.

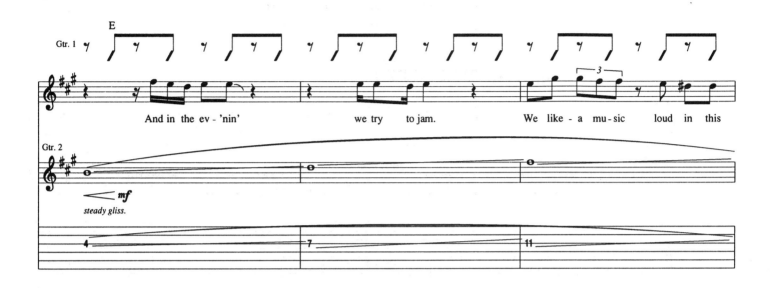

And in the ev - 'nin'   we try to jam.   We like - a mu - sic loud in this

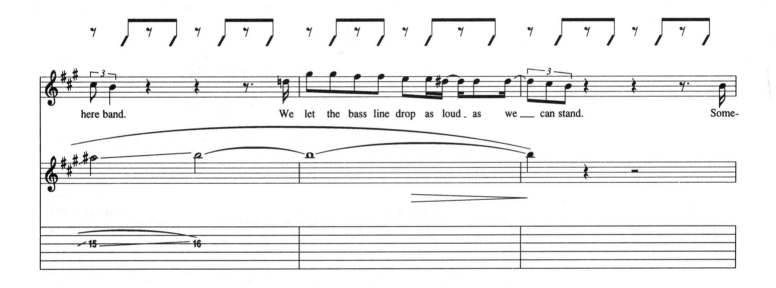

here band.   We let the bass line drop as loud _ as we __ can stand.   Some-

bod-y al-ways got - ta turn in - for - ma for the man.   I wan-na know, know __

* Position slide where imaginary frets
would be (above lead pick up).

right now.   Is there one of   you __   in __ the crowd?

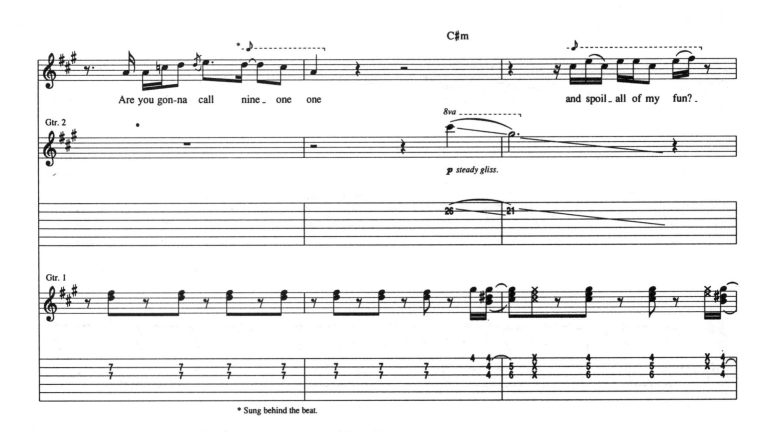

C#m

Are you gon-na call   nine __ one one   and spoil __ all of my   fun? __

Gtr. 2

p steady gliss.

Gtr. 1

* Sung behind the beat.

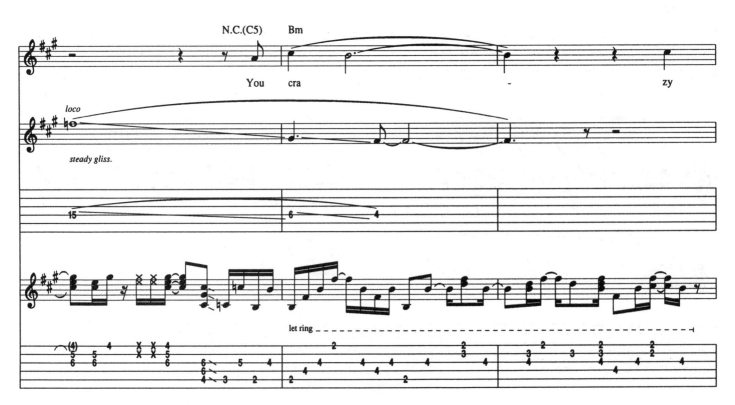

N.C.(C5)   Bm

You   cra   - zy

loco

steady gliss.

let ring

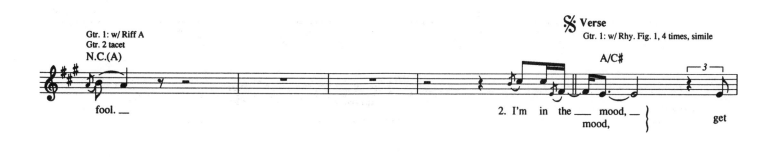

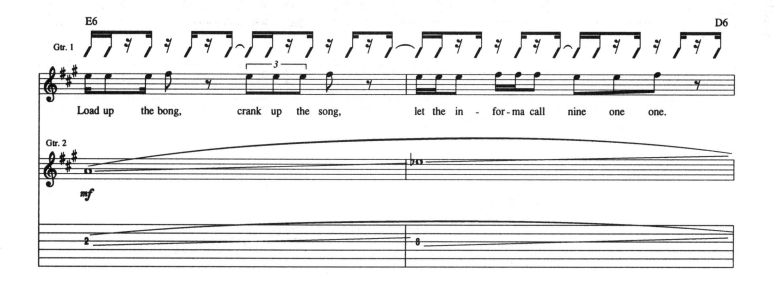

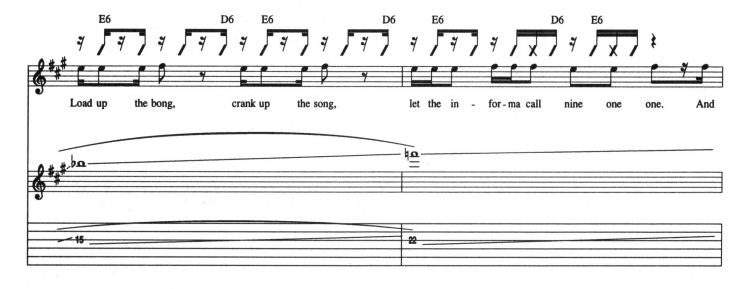

Caress Me Down

Words and Music by Brad Nowell, Eric Wilson and Floyd Gaugh

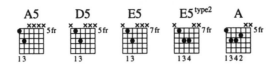

MCA music publishing

And if ___ you wan-na get popped in your knee, just wipe that look off your ba - ti face.

You hate me 'cause I got what you need, a pret - ty lit - tle daugh-ter that we call Mix - ie, yeah.

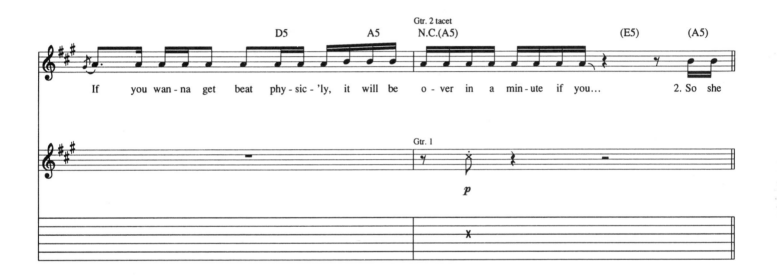

If you wan - na get beat phy - sic - 'ly, it will be o - ver in a min - ute if you... 2. So she

Verse

Gtrs. 1 & 2: w/ Rhy. Figs. 2 & 2A, 2 times, simile

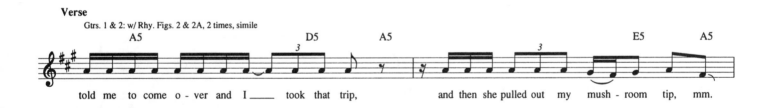

told me to come o - ver and I ___ took that trip, and then she pulled out my mush - room tip, mm.

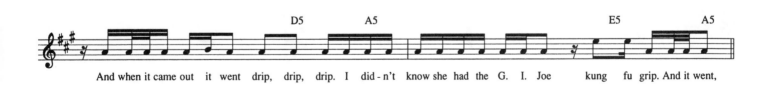

And when it came out it went drip, drip, drip. I did - n't know she had the G. I. Joe kung fu grip. And it went,

Chorus

Gtrs. 1 & 2: w/ Rhy. Figs. 2 & 2A, simile

"Uh!" And the girl ca - ress me down. "Uh," and that's that ___ lov - in' sound. And it went,

Su her-man-na si___ me que-re y a-ho-ri-ta te-ne-mos un be-be. Sus

Gtrs. 1 & 2: w/ Rhy. Figs. 2 & 2A, 4 times, simile

pad-res, sus ti-os me tra-tar-on ma-tar, but they did not get___ too far.___ Um
gus-ta mi reg-gae, me gus-ta punk rock. Pe-ro la co-sa que me gus-ta mas Hi-span-o chi-car. Las

po-co des-pues, tu-ve que re-gre-sar con un chin-go de di-ner-o 'cause you know I'm a star. Mi
nar-gas en el air-e if you know who you are. Por las nar-gas en el air-e em-pi-e-za gri-tar.

vi-da Cos-ta Ri-ca par-a to-mar y su-pe-ar, prac-ti-cu-ba con la ra-za, cause they know who we are. Si
No ten-ga mie-do, I'm___ your pa-pi. Take your cho-nes y los man-den a mi. Le -

no di de la cuen-ta and I'll bet you nev-er were. You must be a mun-e-ca if you're still stand-in' still and we fall.
van-ta, le-van-ta, ti-en-es que gri-tar. Le-van-ta, le-van-ta, ti-en-es que bai-lar. 'Cause

Chorus

Gtr. 1: w/ Rhy. Fig. 2, 2 times, simile

"Uh," ca-ress me down. "Uh," and that's the___ lov-in' sound. We go

Gtr. 2

simile on repeat

To Coda ⊕

"Uh," and the girl ca-ress me down. And that's the lov-in' sound.

P.S._ _ _ _ _ ⌐

What I Got (Reprise)

Words and Music by Brad Nowell

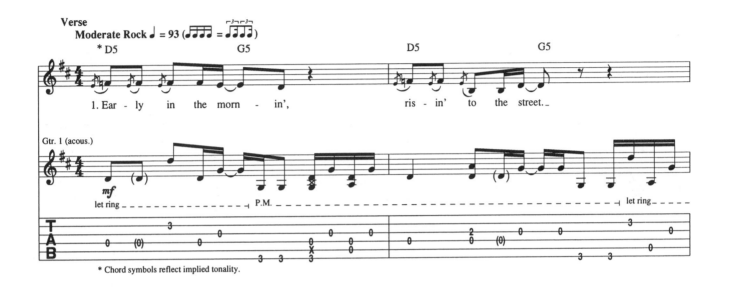

* Chord symbols reflect implied tonality.

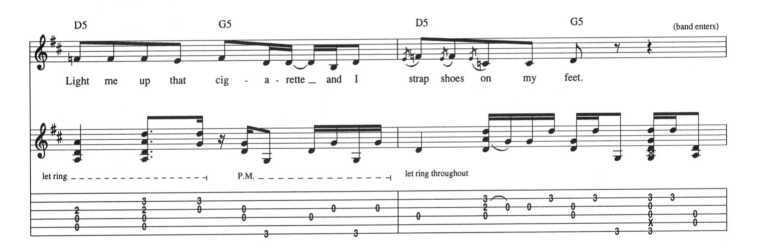

Lov - in' ____ is what I got. ____ I said re - mem - ber that. ____

Interlude

Gtr. 3 tacet

Gtr. 2 tacet

D

Gtr. 2

N.C.(D5) (G5) (D5) (G5)

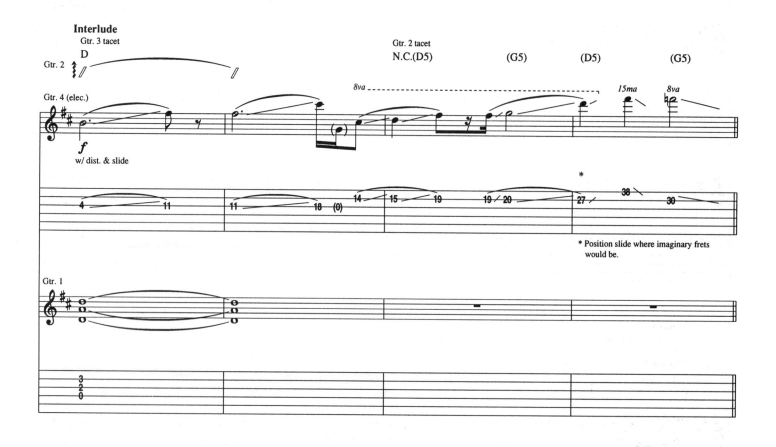

Gtr. 4 (elec.)

f

w/ dist. & slide

8va

15ma 8va

*

* Position slide where imaginary frets
would be.

Gtr. 1

Verse

Gtr. 4 tacet

Gtr. 1: w/ Riff A, 1 3/4 times, simile

D5 G5 D5 G5

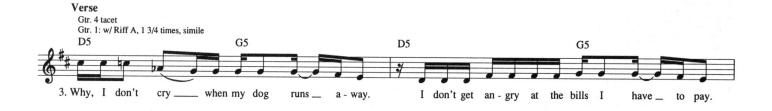

3. Why, I don't cry ____ when my dog runs ____ a - way. I don't get an - gry at the bills I have ____ to pay.

D5 G5 D5 G5

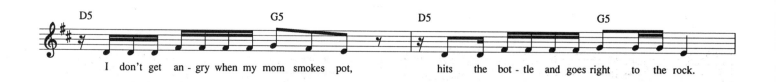

I don't get an - gry when my mom smokes pot, hits the bot - tle and goes right to the rock.

Gtr. 2: w/ Rhy. Fig. 1, 1st 3 meas. only

D

Fuck - in' and fight - in', it's ____ all ____ the same. Liv - in' with Lou - ie Dog's the on - ly way to stay ____ sane.

Doin' Time

Words and Music by Brad Nowell, Marshall Goodman, George Gershwin, Ira Gershwin, Du Bose Heyward, and Dorothy Heyward

* Chord symbols reflect overall tonality.
** Key signature denotes G Dorian.
† Vibraphone arr. for gtr.

Voc. Fill 2

- tion - ship. _

Verse

Gtr. 1: w/ Rhy. Fig. 1, 2 times, 1st & 3rd times.
Gtr. 1: w/ Rhy. Fill 1, 2nd time

1. Me and my girl ____ we got this re - la - tion - ship. ____
2. Oh, ____ take this ____ veil ____ from off ____ my eyes. ____
3. E - vil, I've come to tell you that she's e - vil, most def - i - nite - ly.

I love her so bad, ____ but she treats me like a...
My ____ burn - ing sun will ____ some - day rise. So
E - vil, or - n'ry, scan - dal - ous and e - vil, most def - i - nite - ly. The

On lock down like a pen - i - ten - tia - ry, ____ she spreads her
what am I gon-na be do - in' for a wife? Said I'm gon-na play with my-self.
ten - sion is get - ting hot - ter, I'd like to

lov - in' all ____ o - ver and when ____ she gets home ____ there's none left ____ for me. ____
Show them ____ now we've come ____ off the ____ shelf. ____ So what.
hold her head un - der

3. **Verse**

Gtr. 1 tacet

wa - ter, ____ oh. ____ Me and my girl, we've got a re - la -

Gtr. 2 (clean) **Rhy. Fig. 2** **End Rhy. Fig. 2**

mf

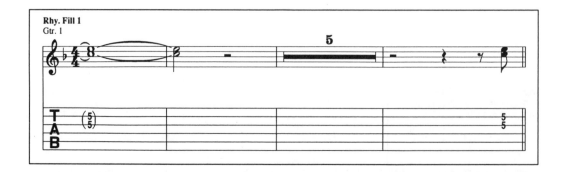

Rhy. Fill 1
Gtr. 1

Gtr. 2: w/ Rhy. Fig. 2, 3 times, simile

-tion - ship, uh.   Me and my ____ girl, ____ hmm, _ we got a re - la-

-tion - ship, mm. ____   My girl, ____   we got a re - la-

w/ Voc. Fill 1   D.S. al Coda

-tion ____ ship,   oh. ____   And my ____ girl, ____   huh, got a re - la-

Coda

Gtr. 1: w/ Rhy. Fig. 1

(Sum - mer - time ____) and the liv-in's ea - sy.

Gtr. 1

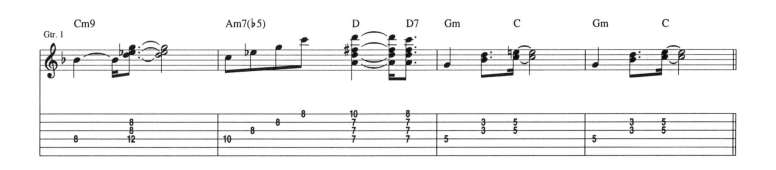

Gtr. 1: w/ Rhy. Fig. 1, 2 times   *Repeat & Fade Out*

Voc. Fill 1

So take a

93

Guitar Notation Legend

Guitar Music can be notated three different ways: on a *musical staff*, in *tablature*, and in *rhythm slashes*.

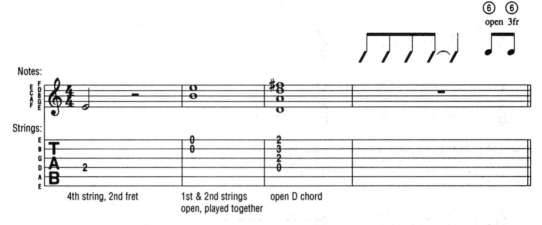

RHYTHM SLASHES are written above the staff. Strum chords in the rhythm indicated. Use the chord diagrams found at the top of the first page of the transcription for the appropriate chord voicings. Round noteheads indicate single notes.

THE MUSICAL STAFF shows pitches and rhythms and is divided by bar lines into measures. Pitches are named after the first seven letters of the alphabet.

TABLATURE graphically represents the guitar fingerboard. Each horizontal line represents a a string, and each number represents a fret.

4th string, 2nd fret

1st & 2nd strings open, played together

open D chord

Definitions for Special Guitar Notation

HALF-STEP BEND: Strike the note and bend up 1/2 step.

WHOLE-STEP BEND: Strike the note and bend up one step.

GRACE NOTE BEND: Strike the note and bend up as indicated. The first note does not take up any time.

SLIGHT (MICROTONE) BEND: Strike the note and bend up 1/4 step.

BEND AND RELEASE: Strike the note and bend up as indicated, then release back to the original note. Only the first note is struck.

PRE-BEND: Bend the note as indicated, then strike it.

PRE-BEND AND RELEASE: Bend the note as indicated. Strike it and release the bend back to the original note.

UNISON BEND: Strike the two notes simultaneously and bend the lower note up to the pitch of the higher.

VIBRATO: The string is vibrated by rapidly bending and releasing the note with the fretting hand.

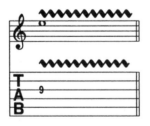

WIDE VIBRATO: The pitch is varied to a greater degree by vibrating with the fretting hand.

HAMMER-ON: Strike the first (lower) note with one finger, then sound the higher note (on the same string) with another finger by fretting it without picking.

PULL-OFF: Place both fingers on the notes to be sounded. Strike the first note and without picking, pull the finger off to sound the second (lower) note.

LEGATO SLIDE: Strike the first note and then slide the same fret-hand finger up or down to the second note. The second note is not struck.

SHIFT SLIDE: Same as legato slide, except the second note is struck.

TRILL: Very rapidly alternate between the notes indicated by continuously hammering on and pulling off.

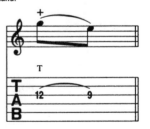

TAPPING: Hammer ("tap") the fret indicated with the pick-hand index or middle finger and pull off to the note fretted by the fret hand.

NATURAL HARMONIC: Strike the note while the fret-hand lightly touches the string directly over the fret indicated.

PINCH HARMONIC: The note is fretted normally and a harmonic is produced by adding the edge of the thumb or the tip of the index finger of the pick hand to the normal pick attack.

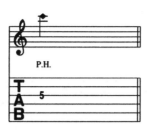

HARP HARMONIC: The note is fretted normally and a harmonic is produced by gently resting the pick hand's index finger directly above the indicated fret (in parentheses) while the pick hand's thumb or pick assists by plucking the appropriate string.

PICK SCRAPE: The edge of the pick is rubbed down (or up) the string, producing a scratchy sound.

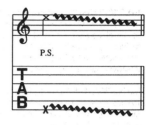

MUFFLED STRINGS: A percussive sound is produced by laying the fret hand across the string(s) without depressing, and striking them with the pick hand.

PALM MUTING: The note is partially muted by the pick hand lightly touching the string(s) just before the bridge.

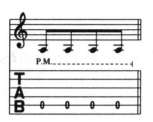

RAKE: Drag the pick across the strings indicated with a single motion.

TREMOLO PICKING: The note is picked as rapidly and continuously as possible.

ARPEGGIATE: Play the notes of the chord indicated by quickly rolling them from bottom to top.

VIBRATO BAR DIVE AND RETURN: The pitch of the note or chord is dropped a specified number of steps (in rhythm) then returned to the original pitch.

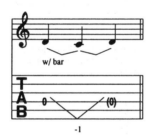

VIBRATO BAR SCOOP: Depress the bar just before striking the note, then quickly release the bar.

VIBRATO BAR DIP: Strike the note and then immediately drop a specified number of steps, then release back to the original pitch.

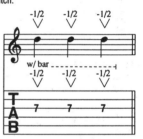

Additional Musical Definitions

 (accent)
- Accentuate note (play it louder)

 (accent)
- Accentuate note with great intensity

 (staccato)
- Play the note short

- Downstroke

∨
- Upstroke

D.S. al Coda
- Go back to the sign (𝄋), then play until the measure marked "*To Coda*," then skip to the section labelled "*Coda.*"

D.S. al Fine
- Go back to the beginning of the song and play until the measure marked "*Fine*" (end).

Rhy. Fig.
- Label used to recall a recurring accompaniment pattern (usually chordal).

Riff
- Label used to recall composed, melodic lines (usually single notes) which recur.

Fill
- Label used to identify a brief melodic figure which is to be inserted into the arrangement.

Rhy. Fill
- A chordal version of a Fill.

tacet
- Instrument is silent (drops out).

- Repeat measures between signs.

- When a repeated section has different endings, play the first ending only the first time and the second ending only the second time.

NOTE: Tablature numbers in parentheses mean:
1. The note is being sustained over a system (note in standard notation is tied), or
2. The note is sustained, but a new articulation (such as a hammer-on, pull-off, slide or vibrato begins, or
3. The note is a barely audible "ghost" note (note in standard notation is also in parentheses).